MW00425253

Table of Contents

Section 1 – Testing
Two-part knowledge exam 3
Road skills test 4
Vision screening 4
    Vision standards 4

Section 2 – Signals, Signs and Pavement Markings
Traffic signals 5
    Lane use signals 6
Traffic signs 6
    Sign colors 6
    Sign shapes 6
    Regulatory signs 7
    Warning signs 8
    Work zones 10
Pavement markings 10
Painted curbs 13

Section 3 – Safe Driving
Hand position 13
Speed limits 14
Stopping 14
Yielding the right-of-way 15
Roundabouts 16
Changing lanes 16
Passing 16
Over-correcting 17
Turning 17
U-turns 17
Turn signals 17
Maintaining a space cushion 18
    Following distance 18

Searching 18
Blind spots 19
Sharing the road 19
    Pedestrians 19
    Bicycles 19
    Mopeds 19
    Motorcycles 19
    Light rail 20
    Low speed vehicles 20
    Trucks, tractor-trailers, buses and RVs 20
    Light to medium trailers 20
Backing 21
Parking 21
Visibility 21
Lights 22
Hazardous conditions 22
    Night driving 22
    Fog 22
    Rain 22
    Snow 22
Dangerous driving behaviors 22
    Aggressive driving 22
    Distracted driving 23
    Drowsy driving 23
    Drinking and driving 23
Traffic crashes 24
Deer hazards 24
Traffic stops 25

Section 4 – Seat Belts, Airbags, and Child Safety Seats
Seat belts 25
Air bags 26
Child safety seats 26

Section 5 – Penalties

License suspension 27
License revocation 27
Conviction-related suspensions and revocations...............27
Other DMV requirements, suspensions and revocations.....28
    Driver Improvement Program 28
    Medical review program 28
    Insurance monitoring program...............................29
    Suspension for failing to satisfy child
    support-related requirements 29
Alcohol and the law 29
    Administrative License Suspension........................29
    Open alcohol containers in vehicles 29
    Transporting children while under the influence
    of alcohol/drugs...29
    Vehicle impoundment 29
    Restitution...29
    Alcohol related violations and penalties
    involving persons under age 21 30

Section 6 – License Types

Learner's permit 31
Driver's license 31
Commercial driver's license 31
School bus driver's license 31
Motorcycle learner's permit 32
Motorcycle driver's license...32
International driver's license 32

Section 7 – Other Important Information

Receiving your license by mail 33
Address Changes..33
New to Virginia...33
Titles, registrations, license plates, decals.........................33
Safety inspections 33
Tire safety inspections..33
Insurance requirements 34
Applying to register to vote 34
Organ, eye and tissue donation...34

Section 8 – Sample Knowledge Exam

Sample exam..35

Section 1:
Testing

The exam may be taken only once per business day. An audio version of the exam is available and the exam is offered in many different languages and American Sign Language. Therefore, translators may not be used for tests in offered languages.

If you fail the knowledge exam three times, you will not be able to take it a fourth time until you complete and pass the classroom component of driver education.

You may have the option of completing an 8-hour course based on the Virginia Driver's Manual and approved by DMV exclusively for satisfying the three-times-failure requirement. This course is available at a driver training school and online. Please see the requirements below based on your age.

- Customers age 18 and older may complete a course based on the Virginia Driver's Manual. The completion date of the driver's manual course must be after the date that you failed the knowledge exam the third time. When you successfully complete the course and give DMV your certificate of completion, you can take the knowledge exam again.

- Customers younger than 18 may complete the course based on the Virginia Driver's Manual if they have previously completed the classroom component of driver education. Before you can take this course, you must present your certificate of completion for the classroom component of driver education to the driver training school that will be conducting the driver's manual course. The completion date of the driver's manual course must be after the date that you failed the knowledge exam the third time. When you successfully complete the course and give DMV your certificate of completion, you can take the knowledge exam again.

When testing, you cannot:
- get help while taking the exam
- help another person taking the exam
- try to get test questions or answers before the exam
- give another person exam questions or answers
- use a cell phone during the exam

A sample knowledge exam is in Section 8 of this manual and at www.dmvNOW.com.

Services for Persons With Disabilities
Customers with special needs or who require special help with applications or testing should tell a DMV staff member at any DMV location.

In this section you'll learn about:
- Two-part knowledge exam
- Road skills test
- Vision screening
  - Vision standards

Tests will include a vision screening and may include a two-part knowledge exam and a road skills test. A DMV representative will tell you which tests you need to take.

Two-Part Knowledge Exam

You will need to take the knowledge exam if you do not hold a valid driver's license from another U. S. state, Canada, Germany, France, or the Republic of Korea. The two-part knowledge exam is given on a computer and tests your knowledge of traffic signs, motor vehicle laws, and safe driving. Exam questions are taken from information in this manual. You must correctly answer all ten traffic sign questions in part one of the exam before you can take part two of the exam. Part two tests your general knowledge with multiple choice questions. You must answer at least 80 percent of these questions correctly to pass part two.

If you fail the exam and you are under age 18, by law you must wait a full 15 days before you can retake the exam. For example, if you fail the exam on January 1, the earliest you can take the exam again is January 17.

Road Skills Test

You will need to take the road skills test if you do not hold a valid driver's license from another U. S. state, Canada, Germany, France, the Republic of Korea, or Taiwan. You must provide a vehicle for the road skills test (cannot be taken in an autocycle). The vehicle must have a valid safety inspection sticker, license plates, registration card and decals, working brakes, safety belts, horn, lights, turn signals, mirrors and speedometer.

To take the road skills test, the DMV examiner will require that you either:

▸ present an acceptable driver's education certificate of completion, or

▸ complete a behind-the-wheel checklist (DMV form CSMA 19 available at www.dmvNOW.com or any DMV office) that describes specific driving tasks that you may be asked to perform while taking the road skills test. A licensed driver will need to certify on the form that he/she has been with you while you practiced the driving tasks and that you have complied with all requirements for learner's permit holders while operating a motor vehicle.

For applicants under 18, the road skills test will be given as part of the driver education course taken at a public, private or commercial driving school. If you are home schooled, refer to the Home-Schooled In-Car Driver Education Information Sheet (HS 3) for more information about taking the road skills test.

Applicants age 18 or older must hold the learner's permit for 60 days prior to the first road skills test or complete a course of driver's education at a driver training school approved by DMV or the Department of Education. For applicants who choose to take driver's education, the road skills test will be administered by the driver training school. For those who opt to hold a learner's permit for 60 days, the road skills test will be given by a DMV staff member. The test may be taken only once per business day. If you fail the road skills test, you must wait two days to take it again. If you fail the road skills test at DMV three times, you will not be able to take it a fourth time until you complete and pass the in-vehicle part of driver education at a driver training school approved by DMV or the Department of Education. The completion date for the in-vehicle part must be after the date you failed the road skills test the third time. Once you successfully complete the in-vehicle part and give DMV your certificate of completion, you can take the road skills test again.

Vision Screening

To screen your vision, a DMV staff member will ask you to look into a machine and read a series of letters or numbers. The vision screening is not a medical exam. The screening shows whether your vision meets Virginia's standards to safely drive. If you fail the vision screening, you may be asked to visit an eye care professional.

If you need to wear glasses or contact lenses to pass the vision screening, you must wear them when you drive. Your license will display a C for this restriction. To have this restriction removed after having laser surgery to correct your vision, you must visit a DMV customer service center and pass the vision screening without wearing glasses or contact lenses or submit a Vision Screening Report (MED 4).

Vision Standards

Driver's license – unrestricted

▸ 20/40 or better vision in one or both eyes, and

▸ 110 degrees, or better, horizontal vision in one or both eyes, or comparable measurement that shows a field of vision within this range.

Driving – restricted to daylight hours only

▸ 20/70 or better vision in one or both eyes, and

▸ 70 degrees, or better, horizontal vision. If you have vision in only one eye, you must have horizontal vision of at least 30 degrees or better when looking toward your nose and 40 degrees or better when looking toward your temple, or comparable measurement that shows a field of vision within this range.

A daylight driving only restricted license permits you to drive only during the period of time beginning a half-hour after sunrise and ending a half-hour before sunset.

Bioptic telescopic lenses: If you wear bioptic telescopic lenses, read the DMV publication Driver's Licensing Information for Bioptic Telescopic Lense Wearers (MED 44) available at www.dmvNOW.com or contact DMV at (804) 497-7100.

Section 2:
Signals, Signs and Pavement Markings

You may not turn right on red if signs are posted at the intersection that read "No Turn on Red," or if a red arrow pointing to the right is displayed.

Left turn on red: You may turn left at a red light if you are on a one-way street and turning left onto another one-way street while the traffic signal displays a red light. Before turning, you must come to a complete stop. Look both ways and yield the right-of-way to pedestrians and other traffic. Be sure to check for less visible vehicles such as motorcycles, bicycles, and mopeds. **You may not turn left** on red if signs are posted at the intersection that read "No Turn on Red," or if a red arrow pointing to the left is displayed.

Red arrow: A red arrow means you must stop if you intend to move in the direction of the arrow. You may not proceed in the direction of the arrow as long as the red arrow is displayed, unless signs are posted at the intersection that read "Right on Red Arrow After Stop" or "Left on Red Arrow After Stop." Virginia law prohibits right and left turns at red arrow lights.

Note: If you are traveling in another state, make sure you know its laws for right and left turns at red and red arrow lights.

Flashing red light: At a flashing red light, come to a complete stop and yield to oncoming vehicles and pedestrians. You may go when the way is clear. At a railroad crossing, you must come to a complete stop even if you don't see a train.

Flashing red arrow: At a flashing red arrow, come to a complete stop, yield the right-of-way to vehicles coming from the other direction and pedestrians in the intersection, and proceed in the direction of the arrow when the way is clear.

Yellow light or arrow: A yellow light or arrow are cautions warning that the light is about to change. If you have not entered the intersection, stop; or, if unsafe to stop, cautiously go through it. If you are already in the intersection, go through it cautiously. Do not speed up to beat the light.

Flashing yellow light: A flashing yellow light means slow down and proceed with caution. Flashing yellow lights are at locations with higher-than-normal hazardous conditions.

Flashing yellow arrow: At a flashing yellow arrow, you may turn in the direction of the arrow, if the way is clear. Yield the right-of-way to vehicles coming from the other direction and pedestrians in the intersection. Be sure to check for less visible vehicles such as motorcycles, bicycles, and mopeds. If a traffic light changes from red to flashing yellow arrow while a pedestrian is in the intersection, allow the pedestrian to cross the street before turning.

In this section you'll learn about:

▸ Traffic signals
▸ Traffic signs
▸ Pavement markings
▸ Painted curbs

Traffic signals, signs and pavement markings are used for traffic control to provide a smooth, orderly flow of traffic. It is important to understand and obey them. It is illegal to avoid these traffic controls by cutting through a parking lot or field.

Obey all signs and signals unless directed by a police officer; always follow the officer's direction.

Traffic Signals

Traffic signals apply to drivers, motorcycle riders, bicyclists, moped-riders and pedestrians.

Red light: At a red light, come to a complete stop at the stop line or, if there is no stop line, before entering the intersection or before reaching the crosswalk. Remain stopped as long as the signal is red, unless turns are allowed.

Right turn on red: You may turn right while the traffic signal displays a red light. Before turning, you must come to a complete stop. Look both ways and yield the right-of-way to pedestrians and other traffic. Be sure to check for less visible vehicles such as motorcycles, bicycles and mopeds.

Green light or arrow: At a green light, you may go if the way is clear. At a green arrow, you may go in the direction of the arrow if the way is clear. If you are turning without a green arrow, you must yield the right-of-way to vehicles coming from the other direction and pedestrians in the intersection. Be sure to check for

less visible vehicles such as motorcycles, bicycles, and mopeds. If a traffic light changes from red to green while a pedestrian is in the street, allow the pedestrian to cross the street before turning.

Out of service signals: When traffic signals are not working because of a power outage or other problem and not displaying any lights, you are required to stop, proceeding through the intersection as though it were an all-way stop. This does not apply if a law enforcement officer or other authorized person is directing traffic at the intersection, or if portable stop signs are in use.

Lane use signals indicate lanes where you can and cannot drive during different hours of the day.

Red X: Never drive in a lane marked with a red X signal.

Yellow X or Yellow Diagonal Downward Arrow: These signals mean that you should move out of the lane as soon as safely possible.

Green Arrow: You are permitted to drive in a lane marked with a green arrow signal.

Left-turn Arrow: You are permitted to enter in a lane marked with a one-way or two-way arrow only to turn in the direction of the arrow.

Pedestrian Hybrid Beacons (PHBs): PHBs appear over intersections without stoplights and alert drivers when pedestrians are at a crosswalk. One yellow light at the bottom flashes when a pedestrian activates the PHB. Next, the yellow light turns solid to alert drivers to prepare to stop. Then, the top two red lights on the PHB turn solid while a walk signal appears at the crosswalk, and drivers must stop. Lastly, while the walk signal counts

down for the pedestrians, the PHB's two red lights alternate flashing, telling the driver that if the crosswalk is now clear, they may proceed with caution.

Traffic Signs

The color and shape of a traffic sign communicates important information about the sign's message. In poor visibility conditions, such as heavy fog, you may be able to make out only the shape of a sign. As you approach a sign and while still distant, you may see the color long before you can read the message or see the symbol, giving you some advance information.

Sign Colors

Sign colors help you know what the intention of the sign is.

Red used with white conveys stop, yield, do not, and no. Stop signs, yield signs, do not enter or wrong way signs, the circle and slash in a no turn sign, and the restrictions in a parking sign are examples.

Black used with white conveys regulatory information. Speed limit, do not pass, no turns are examples where the operation is regulated by law and the black and white sign would be found.

Yellow used with black conveys a warning. Curve ahead, stop ahead, overhead clearances, slippery when wet, are all examples. A specialized class of warning signs uses a strong yellow/green color with black to advise of school zone, pedestrian and/or bicyclist activities.

Green and white, blue and white, and brown and white signs are used to provide helpful information. The green sign is used to provide destination types of information, while the blue sign is used to inform regarding motorists services. The brown sign is used to advise of historical or cultural interests that might exist in the area.

Orange and black and pink and black signs are used to advise and warn in construction (orange) and incident (pink) areas. They are used with black and white signs that convey regulations that might exist only because of the construction effort or the incident.

Sign Shapes

Octagon (Stop): This eight-sided shape always means stop. You must come to a complete stop at the sign, stop line, pedestrian crosswalk or curb. Wait for any

vehicle or pedestrian to clear the way. At some intersections you'll find a sign beneath the stop sign that reads "All Way" or "4 Way." At these intersections all vehicles on all roads leading into the intersection must stop. If you get to the intersection at the same time as other vehicles, the driver on the left must yield to the driver on the right.

Triangle (Yield): You must slow down as you come to the intersection. Be prepared to stop. Let any vehicles, pedestrians or bicyclists safely pass before you proceed.

Rectangle (Regulatory or Guide):
Vertical signs generally give
instructions or tell you the law.
Horizontal signs may give directions
or information.

Diamond (Warning): These signs warn
you of special conditions or hazards ahead.
Slow down and drive with caution. Be ready
to stop.

Pentagon (School Zone/School Crossing):
This five-sided shape marks
school zones and warns you
about school crossings. Two
signs may be used together to
show the actual location of the
crosswalk.

Regulatory signs inform you of the law;
you must obey their instructions. Remember
that a red circle with a slash means NO —
the symbol inside the circle tells you what is
prohibited.

Speed Limit: These signs tell you the maximum legal speed
that you may drive on the road where the sign is posted when
weather conditions are good. Some roads
have electronic speed limit signs that change
based on weather or traffic conditions. During
rain, snow and ice, you may receive a ticket
for driving too fast for the conditions even
if you are driving at or less than the posted
speed limit.

Do Not Enter – Wrong Way: These signs mean you cannot
drive in that direction. If you drive past these
signs you are going in the
wrong direction and could
get into a head-on crash with
vehicles headed your way.
Cautiously turn around.

One Way: Traffic flows only
in the direction of the arrow.

No Left Turn: Left turns are against the law.
In Virginia, U-turns are considered as two left
turns and are illegal if this sign is posted.

No Right Turn: Right turns are illegal. Do not
make a right turn when you see this sign.

No U-Turn: U-turns are illegal. Do not make
a U-turn when you see this sign.

No Turn on Red: You may not turn on the
red light. Wait for the signal to turn green.

Do Not Pass: This sign marks the beginning
of a no passing zone. You may not pass cars
ahead of you in your lane, even if the way is
clear.

Left Turn Yield on Green: This sign is used
with a traffic signal. It tells you that the traffic
turning left at a green light does not have the
right-of-way and must yield to traffic coming
from the other direction. Stop and look for
oncoming traffic, then proceed with caution.

Keep Right: A traffic island, median or barrier is
ahead. Keep to the side indicated by the arrow.

Lane Use Control: These
signs are used where turns are
required or where special turning
movements are permitted for
specific lanes. Traffic in the lane
must turn in the direction of
the arrow.

High Occupancy Vehicle: These signs
indicate lanes reserved for buses and
vehicles with a driver and one or more
passengers as specified on the sign.

Disabled Parking: Parking spaces marked
with these signs are reserved for people with
disabled parking permits.

Warning signs alert you to possible hazards ahead. Slow down and watch for other pavement markings, signs, signals or work zones that may follow.

Advisory Speed: This sign indicates the maximum safe speed for a highway exit.

Reduced Speed Limit Ahead: Prepare to reduce your speed; the speed limit is changing ahead.

Stop Ahead/Yield Ahead: A stop sign or yield sign is ahead. Slow down and be ready to stop.

Signal Ahead: Traffic signals are ahead. Slow down and be ready to stop.

No Passing Zone: This sign marks the beginning of a no passing zone. You may not pass cars ahead of you in your lane, even if the way is clear.

Merge: Two lanes of traffic moving in the same direction are about to become one. Drivers in both lanes are responsible for merging safely.

Lane Reduction: The right lane ends soon. Drivers in the right lane must merge left when space opens up. Drivers in the left lane should allow other vehicles to merge smoothly.

Divided Highway Begins: The highway ahead is split into two separate roadways by a median or divider and each roadway is one-way. Keep right.

Divided Highway Ends: The highway ahead no longer has a median or divider. Traffic goes in both directions. Keep right.

Slippery When Wet: When pavement is wet, reduce your speed. Do not brake hard or change direction suddenly. Increase the distance between your car and the one ahead of you.

Low Clearance Sign: The overpass ahead has a low clearance. Do not proceed if your vehicle is taller than the height shown on the sign.

Hill: A steep grade is ahead. Check your brakes.

Deer Crossing: Deer cross the roadway in this area. Slow down, be alert and be ready to stop.

Horse-Drawn Buggies: Regularly travel in this area. Slow down and don't use the horn. State law requires motorists to pass with at least three feet of clearance when the way is clear.

Tractors and Farm Equipment: Regularly travel in this area. Be ready to slow down or stop. Only pass when the way is clear.

Pedestrian Crossing: Watch for people entering a crosswalk or crossing your path. Slow down and be prepared to stop. A second sign with an arrow may show the actual location of the crosswalk.

Bicycle Crossing/Bike Path: Bicycles regularly cross or ride beside traffic in this area. Drive with caution. A second sign with an arrow may show the actual location of the bike crossing.

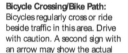

School Zone/School Crossing: Watch out for children crossing the street or playing. Be ready to slow down or stop. Obey speed limits and signals from any crossing guards. A second sign with an arrow may show the actual location of the sidewalk.

Open Joints: Slow down. Open joints on bridges or ramps could cause a motorcyclist to lose control of the motorcycle.

Expansion Joints: This sign is used when a joint across lanes creates a bump or is wide enough to cause loss of traction in wet weather.

Intersections: An intersection is ahead. Be alert for vehicles entering the road on which you are traveling.

Y Intersection: You must bear either right or left ahead.

T Intersection: The roadway you are traveling on ends ahead at a stop sign. You must turn right or left after yielding to oncoming traffic and pedestrians.

Roundabout: These signs indicate a circular intersection with an island in the center is ahead. Also called traffic circles, these intersections may have one or more lanes. Entering traffic must yield the right-of-way to traffic already in the circle and travel in a counter clockwise direction.

Right Curve – Side Road: The road ahead curves right and a side road joins from the left within the curve. Be alert for vehicles entering the roadway you are traveling on.

Sharp Right Turn: Slow down and be prepared for a sharp right turn in the road ahead.

Sharp Right and Left Turns: Slow down and be prepared for the road ahead to turn sharply right, then left.

Right and Left Curves: The road ahead curves right, then left. Slow down.

Right Curve with Safe Speed Indicator: The road ahead curves right. Slow down to the safe speed indicated.

Winding Road: The road ahead winds with a series of turns or curves. On all curves, slow down for better control.

Low Ground Railroad Crossing: A steep slope where the railroad tracks cross the road may cause the bottom of low vehicles to get caught or drag on the tracks.

Railroad Crossing: Advance warning signs are placed before a railroad crossing. These signs warn you to look, listen, slow down and be prepared to stop for trains or any vehicles using the rails.

Railroad Crossbuck: This sign is a warning of a railroad crossing. Look, listen, slow down and be prepared to stop for trains or any vehicles using the rails. Trains may be approaching from either direction. If there is more than one track, trains may be approaching from either direction on either track.

Railroad Crossbuck and Flashing Lights: Flashing lights may be used with crossbuck signs. Always stop when the light begins to flash and be alert for approaching trains. Do not proceed until all trains or any other vehicles using the rails have passed, the tracks are clear, and the lights are no longer flashing. Be especially alert at multi-track crossings because a second train could be approaching from the opposite direction.

Crossbuck, Flashing Lights and Gate: Gates are used with flashing light signals at some crossings. Stop when the lights begin to flash and before the gate lowers. Remain stopped until the gates are raised and the lights stop flashing. Do not attempt to drive around the lowered gate.

Pavement markings, consisting of an X and RR, may be painted on the pavement at the approach to some crossings. When approaching railroad tracks, be alert. Trains may approach the crossing at any time and from either direction. Unless you can clear the tracks completely, never start across the tracks. Make sure there is room for your vehicle on the other side of the tracks before proceeding.

7

Note: School buses must always stop at railroad crossings, even when the lights are not flashing.

If a dangerous condition exists at a rail crossing, call the number listed on the emergency sign. This will allow the rail company to stop or reroute approaching rail traffic until the hazard is removed. Be sure to give the posted crossing number so that the hazard can be identified correctly.

REPORT EMERGENCY
TO 1-800-555-5555
CROSSING #221-6200
ON WENDOVER ROAD

If your car stalls on the tracks, don't hesitate. Get out of the car right away and run diagonally away from the tracks in the direction of the oncoming train.

In a work zone, the lives of highway workers depend on drivers like you obeying the posted speed limits and avoiding distractions. If you are convicted of exceeding the speed limit in a highway work zone, you may be fined up to $500. If you are convicted of using a handheld communications device in a highway work zone, you will be fined $250. Remember, the color orange marks a work zone and means slow down and be alert.

Rough Road, Bump, or Uneven Lanes: These signs are used when certain road conditions, such as loose gravel or road construction, affect the roadway surface and create potentially difficult conditions for motorists, especially motorcyclists.

Road Construction Ahead – Detour: These signs indicate a change in the traffic pattern or route ahead. Slow down. Unusual or potentially dangerous conditions are ahead.

Flashing Arrow Boards: Large flashing arrow boards or flashing message signs in work zones direct drivers to proceed into different traffic lanes and inform them that part of the road ahead is closed.

Flaggers: Flaggers are highway workers who normally wear orange or yellow vests, or yellow-green shirts or jackets. They use STOP/SLOW paddles or red flags to stop or direct traffic through the work zone, and to let other workers or construction vehicles cross the road.

Photo Speed Enforcement: This sign indicates that automated photo enforcement is in place for speeding in a work zone. Always obey the posted speed limit in a work zone.

Traffic Control Devices:
Barricades, vertical signs, concrete barriers, drums and cones are the most common devices used to guide drivers safely through work zones. When driving near the devices, keep your vehicle in the middle of the lane and obey the posted speed limit. As you leave the work zone, stay in your lane and maintain your speed. Don't change lanes until you are completely clear of the work zone.

Message Boards: You may see portable or permanent message boards along roadways. They provide information about traffic, road, weather or other hazardous conditions. Always obey any directions posted on these message boards. For information about road conditions or road construction in advance of your trip, visit www.virginiadot.org, www.511virginia.org or call 511.

Rumble Strips Ahead signs warn motorists of black or orange strips placed across the travel lanes in advance of work zones, including a flagger or lane closure. Rumble strips should be slowly driven over, not swerved around.

Slow Moving Vehicles traveling at 25 MPH or less, such as farm equipment, horse-drawn vehicles or highway work vehicles, must display these signs when using a public highway. Be prepared to adjust your speed or position when you see a vehicle with one of these signs.

Pavement Markings

Road markings guide and warn drivers as well as regulate traffic. Markings may be red, yellow or white. They may be used alone or in combinations. Each has a different meaning.

Red markings are generally not used; but, some communities do use red curbs to indicate no parking zones.

Red reflectors on the pavement show areas not to be entered or used. They are positioned on the road surface so that only traffic flowing in the wrong direction would observe them.

Yellow center lines mean two-way traffic, flowing in opposite directions.

Broken yellow center lines mean that passing on the left is allowed in either direction when the way ahead is clear.

A broken yellow line alongside a solid yellow line means that passing is allowed from the side of the broken line, but not from the side of the solid line.

Vehicles on the solid yellow line side may only cross the line to pass pedestrians, bicyclists, and riders of scooters or skateboards, when the opposite lane is clear and you can pass safely.

Double solid yellow lines mark the center of the road and separate traffic traveling in two different directions. Passing is not allowed in either direction. You may not cross the lines unless you are making a left turn or passing pedestrians, bicyclists, and riders of scooters or skateboards, when the opposite lane is clear and you can pass safely.

Broken white lines separate lanes of traffic going in the same direction. You may change lanes with caution.

Dotted white lines are actually small rectangles in a series where each is closely spaced to the next. They are used to show lane assignment in intersections and interchanges where there might otherwise be a tendency to drift out of a lane or an area of intended use. Often they are used to guide two turning lanes through the intersection. Dotted white lines are also used to denote the opening of a turn lane at an intersection and entrance/exit lanes at interchanges.

Many two-lane roads in Virginia **do not have lane markings** to separate the lanes. On an unmarked two-lane road, you may pass a slow moving vehicle on the left side if there are no signs prohibiting passing. Make sure that the way is clear.

Solid white lines show turn lanes and discourage lane changes near intersections, interchange/on- and off-ramps, and at other locations where lane changes might be dangerous. Solid white lines also mark the right edge of pavement. Arrows used with white lines indicate which turn may be made from the lane. Stop lines, crosswalks and parking spaces also are marked by white lines.

White lane arrows are curved or straight. If you are in a lane marked with a curved arrow or a curved arrow and the word ONLY, you must turn in the direction of the arrow. If your lane is marked with both a curved and straight arrow, you may turn or go straight.

Double solid white lines separate lanes of traffic going in the same direction. Most often they are used to designate special use lane from conventional lanes, as when used to separate a High Occupancy Vehicle lanes from the other lanes of an expressway. You may not cross these lines. You may enter the designated special use lane only where signs and markings allow.

Yield line is a line of triangles extending across the roadway that may be used with a yield sign to show the point at which you must yield or stop, if necessary. A yield line is often seen at the entrance of a roundabout.

Bicycle boxes are painted on the road at intersections. They contain a white bicycle symbol. Bike boxes and the bike lanes approaching and leaving

the box may be painted green. Drivers must stop for a red traffic signal behind all bicycle boxes, not inside the box. Bicycle riders will move into the box in front of drivers at the intersection. Right turns on red are not allowed at these intersections. If turning right on a green light, drivers must signal and yield to bicycles on the right.

On three-lane roads with traffic moving in both directions, road markings show when drivers may use the center lane for making left turns or for passing.

If the center lane is marked by a single broken yellow line on both sides, drivers traveling in either direction may use the center lane for passing.

If both sides of the center lane are marked by a solid yellow line and a broken yellow line, drivers traveling in either direction may use the lane for making left turns. However, they may not travel further than 150 feet in this lane.

A shared lane marking, or sharrow, consists of a bicycle symbol with a double chevron arrow above it and is used on travel lanes too narrow for motor vehicles and bicycles to share side-by-side. Sharrows clarify where bicyclists are encouraged to ride in the lane and remind drivers to expect bicyclists on the road.

Bicycle lanes are indicated by a solid or dashed white line or green pavement markings, and a bicyclist symbol. A bicycle lane is for the preferential use of bicyclists. Drivers should not drive in the bicycle lane except when necessary to turn left or right. Before turning, check your mirrors for bicyclists that may be behind you and yield to bicycles in the lane.

High Occupancy Vehicles (HOV) lanes are marked on highways by a diamond shape in the center of the lane. HOV lanes may also be special lanes separated by a barrier or solid double white lines. During heavy traffic periods, HOV lanes are reserved for buses, vanpools, carpools, other high occupancy vehicles, motorcycles, and certain clean special fuel vehicles. Road signs show the minimum number of passengers a vehicle must carry (excluding motorcycles and clean fuel vehicles) to

use the HOV lanes and the times that HOV restrictions are in effect. If the lanes are separated by a barrier, they are reversible. This means that during certain times of the day, traffic flows one way. During other times of the day, traffic flows in the opposite direction. A diamond-shaped marking may also indicate that the lane is reserved for use as a bus lane.

Toll Plazas and Lanes

All toll facilities in Virginia accept payment using E-ZPass toll transponders. Transponders allow drivers to pay electronically without having to stop to pay with cash. If you

have a transponder, as you approach a toll plaza look for and follow signs with the purple E-ZPass logo. If you do not have a transponder, as you approach a toll plaza, look for and follow signs for cash only lanes.

Slow down as you approach toll plazas. Be extra cautious as you approach, enter, and depart toll plazas. There may be other drivers changing lanes and/or toll employees crossing the lanes.

Some toll roads have high speed lanes reserved for vehicles with E-ZPass transponders. Do not enter those lanes unless you have a transponder. However, if you do enter one of those lanes by mistake, do not stop. Stopping is unsafe and could cause a rear-end crash. Cameras will photograph the car's license plate number and the registered vehicle's owner will be billed for the toll.

A painted curb means that you must follow special rules to park there. Check with the locality for specific meanings. Generally, the colors on the curb mean:

White — Stop only long enough to pick up or drop off passengers.

Yellow — Stop only long enough to load or unload. Stay with your car.

Red — Do not stop, stand or park.

Section 3:
Safe Driving

Every time you get behind the wheel, you accept responsibility for your actions. You must obey Virginia's traffic laws, and ensure the safety of you, your passengers, and other motorists, pedestrians and bicyclists on the roadways.

In this section you'll learn about:
▸ Hand position
▸ Speed limits
▸ Stopping
▸ Yielding the right-of-way
▸ Roundabouts
▸ Changing lanes
▸ Over-correcting
▸ Turning
▸ U-turns
▸ Turn signals
▸ Maintaining a space cushion
▸ Searching
▸ Blind spots
▸ Sharing the road
▸ Backing
▸ Parking
▸ Visibility
▸ Lights
▸ Hazardous conditions
▸ Dangerous driving behaviors
▸ Traffic crashes
▸ Deer hazards
▸ Traffic stops

Hand Position

Sit straight but relaxed and place your hands on the steering wheel. If your steering wheel were a clock, your hands should be at the 8 o'clock and 4 o'clock positions. Hold the wheel with your fingers and thumbs. Avoid gripping it with your palms.

Speed Limits

A speed limit is the maximum legal speed you can travel on a road under ideal conditions. You may drive slower than the speed limit, as long as you don't impede the normal movement of traffic, but it is illegal to drive any faster. By law you must drive slower where signs indicate a school zone speed limit or work zone speed limit is in effect, and/or if conditions such as road construction or bad weather make the posted speed unsafe. According to Virginia law, if you are driving 20 or more miles per hour (MPH) above the speed limit, or over 85 MPH, a law enforcement officer may charge you with reckless driving, regardless of the speed limit. It is considered a misdemeanor criminal offense if convicted of reckless driving. The court may require a fine, suspend your driving privilege and/or impose a jail sentence. If the violation results in death and the operator's license was suspended or revoked at the time of the offense, it may be considered a felony, which carries more serious consequences. You are subject to an additional $100 fine if convicted of driving between 81 and 85 MPH in a 65-MPH zone. It is illegal to use radar detectors in Virginia.

Unless there is a speed limit sign stating otherwise, the maximum speed limit for passenger vehicles and motorcycles is 25 MPH for school, business and residential areas; 35 MPH for unpaved roads and 55 MPH for all other roads. Some school zones may have automated photo enforcement, as indicated by signs with the message "Speed Photo Enforced" or similar.

Stopping

You must always stop your vehicle:

- at all stop signs, red traffic lights and flashing red signals
- when entering a street or crossing over a sidewalk from a driveway, alley, building or parking lot
- at railroad crossings with flashing signals
- when signaled by flaggers directing traffic
- for pedestrians attempting to cross the street at a crosswalk
- at the direction of a police officer. If you don't obey a law enforcement officer's signal to stop and the officer pursues you and is killed as a direct result of the pursuit, you will be guilty of a Class 4 felony.
- at the scene of a crash in which you are involved

When approaching a stop sign and the car in front of you proceeds, stop at the sign and proceed when the way is clear.

Stopping for School Buses

In the following pictures, the red vehicles must stop and remain stopped until all children are clear of the roadway and the bus moves again.

- You must stop for stopped school buses with flashing red lights and an extended stop sign when you approach from any direction on a highway, private road or school driveway. Stop and remain stopped until all persons are clear and the bus moves again.
- You must also stop if the bus is loading or unloading passengers and the signals are not on.

- You do not have to stop if you are traveling in the opposite direction on a roadway with a median or barrier dividing the road and the bus is on the opposite side of the median or barrier. However, be prepared for unexpected actions by persons exiting the school bus.

Stopping Distance

Three factors determine the distance that it takes to stop your vehicle: perception time, reaction distance and braking distance.

Perception time: The time it takes you to recognize a hazard.

Reaction distance: The distance your vehicle travels between the time you recognize a problem and the time you apply the brakes.

Braking distance: The distance your car travels after you apply the brakes.

Perception time, reaction distance and braking distance are affected by weather, visibility, and your mental and physical condition. Braking distance is also affected by how fast your vehicle is traveling, the condition of your brakes and tires, and the pavement condition. For example, wet pavement can double your braking distance.

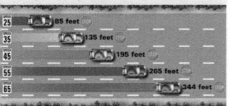

Average stopping distance on dry, level pavement.

Source: Code of Virginia Section 46.2-880

Antilock Brakes

If your vehicle has antilock brakes, be sure that you understand how they work. Check your vehicle owner's manual and practice braking before you go out on the road. Remember, never pump antilock brakes.

Yielding the Right-of-Way

Yield also means to stop if you cannot merge safely into the flow of traffic.

Examples of yielding the right-of-way:

▸ When vehicles from different directions arrive at an intersection at different times, the vehicle that arrives first goes first.

▸ When vehicles from different directions arrive at the same time at an intersection with no signs or signals, the driver on the left must allow the driver on the right to go first.

▸ If the traffic lights at an intersection are not working, all vehicles coming to the intersection must stop. The driver on the left must yield to the driver on the right.

▸ Drivers entering an interstate from an entrance ramp must yield the right-of-way to traffic already on the highway.

▸ Drivers entering any intersection or roundabout must yield to traffic already in it.

▸ When entering a roadway from a private road or driveway, you must stop and yield to all traffic and pedestrians.

▸ You must yield to pedestrians or bicyclists who are crossing a street within a clearly marked crosswalk or at an unmarked intersection. Remember that turns on red are especially hazardous to pedestrians. Avoid conflict with pedestrians and bicyclists; permit them to cross the street safely.

▸ You must yield to funeral processions. Do not cut through, join or interfere with a funeral procession. Unless led by a police escort, the lead vehicle in a funeral procession must obey all traffic signs and signals. Other drivers in the procession may follow carefully without stopping and may use hazard lights (flashers) to indicate they are in the procession.

▸ You must yield to all military convoys. Never cut through or join a military convoy.

Yielding to Vehicles with Flashing Lights

Drivers must take specific actions when they see vehicles with flashing or blinking blue, red, amber (yellow) or white lights on roadways.

Stationary (Stopped) vehicles

▸ When approaching a stationary emergency vehicle or tow truck with flashing lights on a highway, proceed with caution and, if reasonable, with due regard for safety and traffic conditions, change to a lane not next to the vehicle. If you are unable to safely change lanes, reduce your speed and proceed with caution. Violations can result in court suspension of your driver's license and demerit points on your driving record.

▸ When passing stationary vehicles in the process of trash collection on a highway of at least four lanes, change to a lane not next to the vehicle, if you can change lanes safely. If on a highway of fewer than four lanes or if you are unable to change lanes, slow down to 10 miles per hour below the posted speed limit and pass at least two feet to the left of the vehicle.

▸ When passing a stationary mail vehicle, proceed with caution and maintain a safe speed for highway conditions.

▸ You may not park within 500 feet of where fire trucks or equipment are stopped answering an alarm.

Approaching vehicles – same direction

▸ Never follow an emergency vehicle closer than 500 feet when its lights are flashing.

▸ When police, fire and rescue vehicles or ambulances approach you from behind your vehicle using a siren, flashing lights or both, you must immediately yield the right-of-way. Safely pull over to the right edge of the road and stop until the emergency vehicle has passed.

Approaching vehicles – opposite direction

▸ When emergency vehicles approach you in the opposite lane on an undivided highway, you must pull over to the edge of the road and stop until the emergency vehicle passes.

These requirements do not apply in highway work zones.

Roundabouts

Roundabouts are circular intersections with an island in the center and have one or more lanes. Entering traffic must yield the right-of-way to pedestrians, and to traffic already in the circle. Each road approaching the roundabout is marked with a yield sign and may also have yield line markings on the pavement. Drivers must pay attention and obey the signs. After entering the roundabout, drivers must travel in a counter-clockwise direction.

When approaching a roundabout, slow down. Use your turn signals to indicate where you want to go. If you plan to turn right, stay to the right as you enter the roundabout. If you plan to go straight, you may stay in either lane (if it is a dual lane circular intersection). If you plan to turn left, stay to the left as you enter the roundabout.

More information about driving safely through a roundabout is available at the Virginia Department of Transportation web site at http://www.virginiadot.org/info/faq-roundabouts.asp.

Tips for driving safely through a roundabout:

▸ As you approach the roundabout, slow down; look for the street and direction signs. This will help you know which exit to take. These signs should be posted along the roadside before you reach the roundabout.

▸ When you arrive at the roundabout, yield the right-of-way to pedestrians and bicyclists. You also must yield to any vehicles already in the roundabout. Sometimes your entry point will be controlled by a stop or yield sign, or traffic signal. When the way is clear, you may enter the roundabout.

▸ While inside the roundabout, stay in your lane until you are ready to exit. Use your vehicle's right turn signal to let drivers around you know what you want to do.

▸ Do not change lanes or take an exit before checking for vehicles that may be continuing through the roundabout in the lane next to you or behind you. Expect vehicles to be in blind spots you cannot see in your rearview or side mirrors. Quickly glance over your shoulder and check for any vehicles that may be in your blind spot.

Changing Lanes

Before changing lanes, check your side and rearview mirrors for traffic approaching you from behind. Then, use your turn signal to let other drivers know you plan to change lanes. Check for other drivers who also may be moving into the same lane. Just before you begin moving into the other lane, quickly glance over your shoulder and check for any vehicles that may be in your blind spot.

Whether you are changing lanes, passing, entering or exiting a highway, always use your turn signals and check traffic to the rear and sides. When driving on a multi-lane highway, stay in the right lane if you are driving slower than the traffic around you. The left lane is for passing only.

Passing

When passing another vehicle:

▸ check the traffic ahead of you, behind you and in your blind spot before you attempt to pass. Signal and then accelerate to pass. Return to the right lane as soon as you can see the front of the passed vehicle in your rearview mirror.

▸ it is against the law to exceed the speed limit as you pass.

▸ complete the pass before you reach a No Passing zone. If you're still in the left lane when you reach the zone, you're breaking the law.

▸ you may pass on the right if the vehicle you are passing has signaled and is making a left turn. Be cautious because the vehicle you are passing may be blocking your view or blocking the view of other drivers. You may not pass on the right if you must drive off the pavement or main portion of the roadway to get around the other vehicle.

▸ when approaching or passing a person riding a bicycle, moped, or power-assisted bicycle or other device, reduce speed and pass at least three feet to the left.

When being passed, don't speed up. Maintain a steady speed or slow down.

Passing is unlawful and unsafe:

▸ on hills, curves, at intersections or railroad crossings, except on roads with two or more lanes of traffic moving in the same direction

▸ off the pavement or on the shoulder of the road

▸ when a school bus is stopped to load or unload passengers on a public road (unless a physical barrier or unpaved median separates traffic going in either direction) or on a private road

▸ when a solid line marks the left side of your lane

▸ when approaching a crosswalk and the vehicle ahead of you or the lane next to you is stopped

Over-correcting

Over-correcting occurs when the driver turns the steering wheel more sharply than expected, causing the rear wheels of the vehicle to slide toward the outside of the turn. This may result in the loss of vehicle control.

Most over-correction crashes are single vehicle crashes and are often preventable. A driver should remain alert at all times. Reduce speed and use extra caution while driving on curved roads. If you veer off the road, curved or straight, do not panic. Gradually reduce your speed, look in the direction you want to go, slowly steer back onto the roadway.

Turning

To make a right turn you should be in the lane furthest to the right. Signal your intent to turn by using the proper turn signal. You should signal at least three or four seconds, 100 feet, ahead of the turn. Look to your left and right to check the intersection for pedestrians and traffic. Then brake smoothly before and during the turn. If there is a red traffic light or a stop sign at the intersection, come to a complete stop before you make the turn. Turn into the lane closest to the curb unless pavement markings lead you otherwise, and then change lanes if needed.

To make a left turn you should be in the furthest left lane possible, turning into the leftmost lane on the intersecting road, unless pavement markings lead you otherwise; or, unless multiple left turn lanes are provided. If multiple left turn lanes are provided, you should choose the lane that will best serve your need once you enter the intersecting road. Signal your intent to turn by using the proper turn signal. You should signal at least three to four seconds, 100 feet, ahead of the turn. Look in all directions, checking the intersection for pedestrians and traffic coming from the opposite direction.

Keep your front wheels pointed straight ahead until you are actually going to make the left turn. This prevents you from being pushed into oncoming traffic if another vehicle crashes into you from behind. When the way is clear, make the left turn, yield to any vehicles (including bicycles and pedestrians) approaching from the opposite direction.

When two vehicles are approaching each other and signaling to turn left, both vehicles should turn in front of each other so that the passenger sides of the vehicles are beside each other.

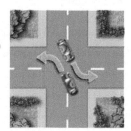

U-Turns

U-turns are not legal everywhere. Before you make a U-turn, check for No U-Turn or No Left Turn signs. In business districts, cities and towns, U-turns are allowed only at intersections. Never make a U-turn on a highway.

When making a U-turn, turn on your left-turn signal, stop, and yield for approaching traffic. When the way is clear, proceed into the outside or right hand lane traveling in the opposite direction.

Turn Signals

When you plan to change lanes, turn, or enter or exit a highway, first give the proper turn signal. Using your turn signal, which is required by law, communicates your intended movement to drivers around you. Develop a good habit and use turn signals or hand signals even if no other traffic is on the road.

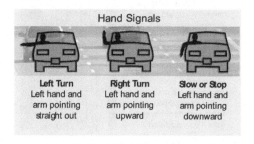

Hand Signals		
Left Turn Left hand and arm pointing straight out	**Right Turn** Left hand and arm pointing upward	**Slow or Stop** Left hand and arm pointing downward

When you plan to turn, signal three or four seconds, 100 feet, ahead of your turn. Be aware that drivers planning to turn into your lane may not know exactly where you will turn; drivers may pull out in front of you. Be alert.

After you complete the turn or lane change, be sure the turn signal stops flashing.

Maintaining a Space Cushion

Space around your vehicle gives you distance to react in emergencies and avoid a crash. Create a space cushion around your vehicle by staying in the middle of your lane. Make sure there is enough room ahead of your vehicle and behind it for other vehicles to pass or stop safely.

Use the two-, three- and four-second rule to determine if you are following far enough behind the vehicle ahead of you.

Following Distance
At these posted speeds and on dry surfaces, this distance, in seconds, allows the driver to steer and brake out of a problem areas.

2 seconds	Under 35 MPH
3 seconds	35-45 MPH
4 seconds	46-70 MPH

Here's how the following distance rule works.

> - Glance at the vehicle ahead as it passes a fixed object, such as an overpass, sign, fence, corner or other fixed mark.
> - Begin counting the seconds it takes you to reach the same place in the road.
> - If you reach the mark before you have counted off two, three, or four seconds, depending on speed, you're following too closely. Slow down and increase your following distance.
> - For bad weather conditions, heavy traffic, poor pavement or if your vehicle is in poor condition, add extra seconds to increase your following distance.

Drivers need to change following distance when speed or road conditions change. Hand response time is close to a half second. Foot response time is normally three-quarters

of a second. This does not take into account any delay in perception time as a result of the driver being tired, on medication, distracted, etc. Road conditions, speed, driver alertness, and the weight of the vehicle you are driving all change the ability to stop.

Increase your following distance when driving:

> - behind a large vehicle that blocks your vision
> - in bad weather or heavy traffic
> - when exiting an expressway
> - behind a motorcycle or bicycle
> - when being tailgated

Tailgating is when the driver behind you is following too closely. If you find yourself in this situation, do not brake suddenly. If possible, move over to another lane, or gently tap your brakes to flash your brake lights and slow down. This should encourage the tailgater to pass you or slow down.

Help the driver behind you by maintaining a safe following distance and a steady speed. Tap your brakes to warn the driver behind you when you plan to slow down or stop.

Searching

Searching means looking at the entire scene for anything that might come into your path. As you search the road, avoid staring at one thing. Keep your eyes moving and learn to read the road and your surroundings.

Looking ahead will help you identify risks early and provide you with more time to react. Expert drivers try to focus their eyes 20 to 30 seconds ahead. In the city, that equals approximately one block. Avoid staring at the middle of the road. Scan from side to side, checking for traffic signs and signals, cars or people that might be in the road by the time you reach them.

Search for clues on the road. Look for exhaust smoke, brake or back-up lights and turned wheels on vehicles. Clues like these warn that the vehicles may pull into your path. Watch for pedestrians, bicyclists and other slow moving vehicles that may be in the road ahead.

When driving in rural areas, watch for hidden intersections and driveways, curves, hills and different road conditions. Watch for other vehicles, especially trucks, oversized and slow-moving farm vehicles, and bicycles.

Check from left to right and then left again before entering an intersection. Whenever you reach a place in the road where other cars, people or animals may cross your path, look both ways to be sure it is clear. These include intersections, crosswalks, shopping centers, construction areas and playgrounds. At any intersection, look to the left first, since cars coming from the left will be closer to you. Then look to the right and take one more quick look to the left before you drive through.

Look behind. Use your rearview mirror to check the traffic behind you frequently, about every 10 seconds. This will alert you if someone is moving up too quickly or tailgating you. Check the traffic behind you when changing lanes, backing up, slowing down quickly or driving down a long, steep hill.

Blind Spots

Blind spots are danger areas where vehicles around you cannot be easily seen. Before driving, adjust your vehicle's mirrors. Make sure the inside rear view mirror frames the entire back window. Adjust both side mirrors so you can barely see the sides of your vehicle.

The best way to see a car in your blind spot is by quickly turning your head and glancing over your shoulder to ensure the way is clear before changing lanes or passing another vehicle.

Avoid driving in someone else's blind spot. This can be just as dangerous as not checking your own blind spot. Speed up or drop back; but, don't stay in the other driver's blind spot.

Sharing the Road

Drivers share the road with many other users: moped and motorcycle riders, trucks and buses, recreational vehicles and other vehicles of all shapes and sizes. Drivers also share the road with vulnerable road users including pedestrians and those on bicycles, wheel chairs, skateboards, roller skates, scooters, animals and animal-drawn vehicles. It is illegal to drive distracted and carelessly around vulnerable road users. It is your responsibility to adjust your driving to avoid others' mistakes and assure everyone's safety.

Pedestrians are especially prone to serious injury when struck.

- Be careful around schools, playgrounds and in residential areas where small children may be playing or crossing the street.

- Look out for the elderly, who may have poor vision and hearing. Remember that the elderly and people with disabilities may move slowly.

- Be especially aware of pedestrians when making a right or left turn. They have the right-of-way. Allow pedestrians to completely cross the street before beginning your turn.

- Passing at a crosswalk is illegal. You may not see pedestrians crossing the road in front of other vehicles.

- Be alert for pedestrians crossing the road. Stop and remain stopped until pedestrians have passed the lane in which your vehicle is stopped.

- Drivers are required to come to a full stop for a pedestrian using a cane or guide dog, as this indicates blindness or vision impairment.

Bicycles: Bicycles are considered vehicles and have the same right-of-way as motor vehicles. Bicyclists are allowed to ride in the center of the lane, when necessary, such as when they are about to turn left or when the lane is too narrow to share side-by-side with a car. Bicyclists are legally allowed on all public roads except interstates and most freeways (limited access highways). Bicyclists may ride no more than two abreast and may not impede the normal flow of traffic. When being overtaken from the rear by a faster-moving vehicle, bicyclists riding side-by-side must move into a single-file formation as soon as they can do so safely. Bicyclists may also be riding in either direction on sidewalks.

Bicycles are subject to many of the same laws as motor vehicles, and bicyclists are subject to many of the same laws as drivers; however, some may not know or obey the rules. Slow down when you approach bicyclists. Using marked bicycle lanes is prohibited by motor vehicles, including while passing. State law requires motorists to pass cyclists with at least three feet of clearance. If the lane is not wide enough to allow for a three-foot clearance, the motorist must change lanes. Give bicyclists plenty of room when passing and be prepared to stop suddenly. Check your blind spots. A bicycle's small size allows it to slip into your blind spot easily. Always check for bicyclists before you pull out, change lanes, turn, back up, open the door, or proceed through an intersection.

Mopeds: It is against the law to operate a moped faster than 35 MPH or on an interstate highway. Any person who operates a moped faster than 35 MPH is considered to be operating a motorcycle which must meet Virginia registration requirements. In addition, the operator would be required to hold a valid driver's license with a motorcycle classification or a driver's license restricted to operating motorcycles only.

Moped riders must be at least age 16 and obey all rules of the road. They must carry some form of government-issued photo identification (does not have to be a driver's license) that includes name, address and date of birth. As a driver, treat moped riders with the same care given to any other vehicle driver.

Riders and passengers must wear helmets, and use eye protection if the moped does not have a windshield. The moped must be titled and registered with DMV.

Although you do not need a driver's license to operate a moped, you may not operate a moped if you have been declared a habitual offender and your license is suspended or revoked for driving while intoxicated.

Motorcycles: Approximately half of all fatal motorcycle crashes involve automobiles. Many crashes are caused by the motorist's failure to see a motorcycle in traffic.

- Look for motorcyclists. In more than half of all crashes involving motorcycles and automobiles, the other driver didn't see the motorcycle until it was too late. Drivers are conditioned to look for four-wheeled vehicles; but they don't expect to see two-wheeled vehicles. A motorcycle's small size also makes it difficult to see.

17

▸ Check your blind spots. A motorcycle's small size allows it to slip into your blind spot easily. Always check for motorcycles before you pull out, change lanes, turn, back up or proceed through an intersection.

▸ Never tailgate a motorcycle (or any other vehicle). Allow yourself plenty of braking distance by adding an extra second to the following distance rule. In inclement weather, double this distance.

▸ Anticipate the motorcyclist's movements. Although a motorcycle is not as wide as the lane, the rider will use the entire lane as traffic situations and road conditions change. A slight change or debris on the road surface can be a major obstacle for a motorcyclist. Expect the motorcycle to make sudden moves within the lane. Never drive beside a motorcycle in the same lane.

▸ Yield to motorcycles. The small size of a motorcycle can cause you to misjudge the motorcycle's speed and distance. Before pulling out into traffic, check twice for motorcycles and use extra caution before you pull out in front of one.

Light Rail: There is a light rail train system in Norfolk called The Tide. Light rail trains share the road with motor vehicles and bicyclists, and they intersect with motor vehicle traffic at 27 locations along the 7.4 mile route. Stay safe when driving around The Tide by obeying the tips below.

▸ Pay attention to changing traffic patterns and always follow the roadway.

▸ Never drive around lowered crossing gates.

▸ Always look both ways before turning across train tracks.

▸ Expect trains on any track at any time.

▸ Always obey signs and traffic signals.

▸ Never stop, pass or shift on train tracks.

▸ Don't cross train tracks unless you have enough room to cross without stopping and can clear the tracks to a safe distance.

For more info about light rail safety, visit www.gohrt.com or call (757) 222-6100.

Low Speed Vehicles: These electrically- or gas-powered four-wheel vehicles have a maximum speed ranging from 21 to 25 MPH. Low speed vehicles may be operated on public roads with speed limits of 35 MPH or less by licensed drivers or learner's permit holders accompanied by a licensed driver. Low speed vehicles must comply with all federal safety standards and must meet Virginia's requirements for passenger vehicle registration and insurance coverage. Golf carts are not classified as low speed vehicles.

Trucks, Tractor-Trailers, Buses and RVs: Trucks, tractor-trailers, buses and recreational vehicles (RVs) – including motor homes, campers and travel trailers – are longer, higher and wider than other vehicles. They accelerate slowly and require greater stopping and turning distances. Plus, there are

danger areas around these vehicles where crashes are more likely to occur. These areas are called No-Zones. No-Zones on the side, front and rear also include blind spots where your car disappears from the driver's view. Learning the No-Zones can save your life.

▸ **Side No-Zones:** Trucks, tractor-trailers, buses and RVs have big No-Zones on both sides that are dangerous because these vehicles must make wide turns. These No-Zones or blind spots are much larger than your car's blind spots. If you can't see the driver's face in his side view mirror, then he can't see you.

▸ **Rear No-Zone:** Trucks, tractor-trailers, buses and RVs have huge No-Zones directly behind them. The driver can't see your car behind his vehicle and you can't see what's happening in traffic ahead of his vehicle. If the truck, bus or RV brakes or stops suddenly, you have no place to go and could crash into the vehicle's rear-end. Always maintain a safe following distance.

▸ **Front No-Zone:** You could get rear-ended by a truck, bus or RV if you cut in front too soon after passing the vehicle or if you cut in front and then suddenly slow down. The truck, bus and RV drivers would be forced to slam on their brakes. These vehicles need nearly twice the time and room to stop as cars. A truck and its trailer may be as long as 65 feet and it may take you more than half a mile of clear road to pass. When passing, look for the entire front of the truck in your rearview mirror before pulling in front. And then, maintain your speed.

▸ **Wide Turns:** Trucks, buses and RVs sometimes need to swing wide to the left or right to safely make a turn. They can't see the cars directly behind or beside them. In fact, their blind spots may stretch up to 20 feet in front of the cab and approximately 200 feet behind the vehicle. Never try to squeeze between a truck, bus or RV and the curb or another vehicle.

Light to Medium Trailers: These trailers are attached to mid-sized cars and trucks with safety chains and a trailer hitch. Large side mirrors are generally needed to increase visibility. Towing a trailer places additional stress on the vehicle; it takes the vehicle twice as long to pass, stop, accelerate and turn. Remember the No-Zones described under Trucks, Tractor-Trailers and RVs.

Before driving a vehicle with a light to medium trailer attached, perform a safety inspection before each trip. Ensure:

▸ the pin securing the ball mount to the receiver is intact

▸ the hitch coupler is secured

▸ safety chains are properly attached

▸ the electrical plug is properly installed

▸ brake lights, turn signals, and license plate lights are functioning properly.

Before pulling a trailer on public roads, find a location such as a vacant parking lot to practice and get the feel for how your vehicle and trailer will handle.

When driving a vehicle with a light to medium trailer attached:

▸ always allow for the added length of the trailer when you change lanes

▸ if your trailer starts to sway, slow down

▸ when backing up, place your hand on the bottom of the steering wheel. If you cannot see where you are backing up, have someone outside to help guide you. To back the trailer to the left, use your left hand to move the wheel left. To back the trailer to the right, use your right hand to move the wheel to the right.

Backing

The most common mistake that drivers make when backing up is failing to look both ways behind them. Mirrors do not give you a full view. To see as much as possible, turn your body and head to the right and look out through the rear window. Back up slowly and check for pedestrians and approaching traffic by glancing quickly to either side.

Parking

When parking on a public road, move as far from traffic as possible. If you park on a shoulder, pull over as far on the shoulder as possible. If you park next to a curb, pull close to it. You may not park more than one foot from the curb. On a two-way street, park on the right side of the road. On a one-way road, park on either side.

Parking on a hill

With a curb: Turn the front wheels of your vehicle to prevent it from rolling into the street.

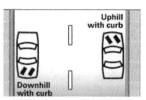

| Parking downhill — with curb Turn front wheels right | Parking uphill — with curb Turn front wheels left |

Without a curb: Turn the front wheels so that if the vehicle rolls, the rear of the vehicle will roll away from traffic.

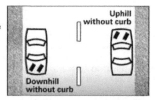

| Parking downhill — no curb Turn front wheels right | Parking uphill — no curb Turn front wheels right |

Be aware of other traffic when exiting your vehicle. Look for other cars, bicyclists, and pedestrians before opening the door.

You may not park:

▸ beside another parked vehicle (double parking)

▸ on crosswalks or sidewalks

▸ in front of driveways

▸ within areas where parking is prohibited by curbs painted yellow or No Parking signs

▸ in a parking space reserved for disabled persons

▸ in striped access aisles adjacent to a parking space reserved for disabled persons

▸ on the hard surface of a road when no curb is present

▸ within 15 feet of a fire hydrant

▸ within 20 feet of an intersection

▸ in a bike lane

▸ within 15 feet of the entrance to a fire, ambulance or rescue squad station

▸ within 500 feet of where fire trucks or equipment are stopped answering an alarm

▸ within 50 feet of a railroad crossing

▸ in such a way that you block or create a hazard for other vehicles in a designated traffic lane

Visibility

Most of what you do while driving depends on what you see. To be a good driver, you need to know what to look for, where to look, and how to adjust to possible problems. The single biggest contributor to crashes is failing to identify a risk. Always know where other vehicles are positioned around you. You must look down the road, to the sides, and behind your vehicle. You must also be alert for unexpected events, especially pedestrians and bicyclists. You must use your headlights at night and at other times when it's hard to see. You must be alert and pay attention to what is going on around you.

Lights

Virginia law requires motorists to use headlights during inclement weather such as rain, fog, snow or sleet when visibility is reduced to 500 feet. You must use your headlights whenever you use your windshield wipers as a result of bad weather. Using headlights at all times, including during the day, increases your vehicle's visibility.

Hazardous Conditions

Driving becomes hazardous when visibility is reduced or when the road surface is covered with rain, snow or ice. Reducing your speed should be your first response to decreased visibility and dangerous road conditions. Increase your space cushion by doubling your normal following distance (refer to the Maintaining a Space Cushion section for more information). Turn on your headlights.

Night Driving

At sunset, as soon as light begins to fade, turn on your headlights to make your vehicle more visible to others. You must use headlights from sunset to sunrise.

Use low-beams when driving in cities and towns, except on streets where there is no lighting. Switch to low-beams whenever you meet oncoming traffic to avoid blinding the other driver. When following, use low-beams whenever you are within 200 feet of the vehicle ahead.

Use high-beam headlights on highways, unless another vehicle is within 500 feet coming toward you. If the high-beams of an oncoming car are on, avoid looking directly at the bright lights. Glance toward the side of the road, then look quickly ahead to determine the other vehicle's position. Keep doing this until you have passed the other vehicle. Even if the other driver does not dim his headlights, do not turn on your high-beam headlights.

Fog

Fog reflects light and can reflect your own headlights back into your eyes. Use low-beam headlights in heavy fog and look for road edge markings to guide you. Even light fog reduces visibility and your ability to judge distances, so slow down.

Rain

Driving in heavy rain can be as hazardous as driving in fog, especially if the wind is blowing. Other vehicles to the rear and in blind spot areas are especially difficult to see when it's raining.

Use your low-beam headlights to see and be seen. In light rain or drizzle, turn on your windshield wipers to improve visibility; using wipers for sprinkles may smear the windshield and make it harder to see, so make sure you have windshield washer fluid.

When rain begins, during the first half-hour, roads are more likely to be slippery due to oil on the road surface mixing with water. Use caution when driving through ponded water, and avoid it if possible. Ponded water can cause vehicles to hydroplane or otherwise lose control.

Snow

Remove snow and ice from your entire car, including the roof, hood and rear of the vehicle, before you start driving. Snow and ice left on the car can fly off when the vehicle is moving and create a hazard for other motorists. Be sure to clear all of your windows, mirrors and front and rear lights of snow or ice so you can see and communicate with other drivers.

Equip your car with all-weather snow tires or chains to help prevent skidding and reduce stopping distance.

Driving on packed snow is similar to driving on ice. When you brake, apply the brakes gently. Slow down before stopping or turning.

When driving on slippery surfaces and you need to stop, release the accelerator and apply brakes gently. You have the most traction and control when the front tires are rolling. Keeping a slow, steady speed – rather than hard braking – will allow you to control your vehicle.

Watch for ice on bridges and in shady areas. Bridges freeze before other road surfaces.

Dangerous Driving Behaviors

Aggressive Driving

This dangerous driving behavior is defined by Virginia law as the intent to harass, intimidate, injure or obstruct another person while committing one or more traffic offenses such as failing to stop or yield the right-of-way, avoiding a traffic control device or failing to give way to an overtaking vehicle.

When aggressive drivers are behind the wheel, these high-risk drivers take out their anger on other motorists. Their frustration levels run high while their concerns for fellow motorists run low. They break the law by running stop signs and red lights, speeding, tailgating, weaving in and out of traffic, passing on the right (including on the shoulder and unpaved portions of the road), making improper and unsafe lane changes, as well as making hand and facial gestures, screaming, honking and flashing their lights.

Protect yourself. If you see an aggressive driver, stay out of the way. Don't challenge the aggressive driver by speeding up or trying to out-maneuver him. Avoid eye contact and ignore his gestures and shouting.

Remember, if you are convicted of aggressive driving, your license could be suspended for ten days or for as long as six months.

Distracted Driving

Driving requires your full attention. There are many distractions that may prevent drivers from focusing on driving: changing the radio or CD, talking to passengers, observing outside surroundings, eating, using a cell phone and more. When on the road, drivers should not use cell phones, computers or other distracting devices except to report a crash or emergency. Before engaging in distracting behavior, pull over and stop the vehicle in a safe location.

Virginia law prohibits drivers from holding cell phones or any other wireless communication devices while driving except in a driver emergency or the vehicle is lawfully parked or stopped. A mobile phone or other telecommunications device may be used for navigation, as long as the driver is not entering information or holding it while driving.

Annually, driver distraction accounts for roughly 20 percent of all traffic crashes in Virginia. Why is distracted driving so deadly? Because while the driver is distracted, the vehicle may move into a high risk situation. The driver then loses precious seconds before recognizing the situation and must make an emergency maneuver. Young distracted drivers are even more susceptible. Failure to maintain proper control, following too closely, and not yielding the right-of-way are common actions of young distracted drivers. Inexperience in handling or controlling a vehicle during an emergency situation combined with distracted driving (cell phone use, other passengers, eyes not on the road, etc.) puts them at greater risk of a crash.

Don't let this happen to you. Take the following precautions.

▸ Concentrate. Keep your eyes on the road and your hands on the wheel at all times. Also, keep your body alert; sit straight, but relaxed. Look in the direction that you want to go.

▸ Set or adjust the controls on the vehicle and other devices as soon as you get in the car and before you begin driving.

▸ Do not use a cell phone.

▸ Anticipate the traffic and environment around you by searching ahead and checking your rearview mirrors often.

▸ Maintain a space cushion around your vehicle. Make sure there is enough room ahead of your vehicle and behind it.

Drowsy Driving

Constant yawning, head nodding, heavy eyelids, difficulty remembering the last few miles driven, missing road signs or exits, unplanned lane changes, driving off the road or hitting rumble strips are all signs of drowsy driving. Driving while you are sleepy increases your crash risk as you struggle to process complex information coming from different places at once. You may make careless driving decisions, have trouble paying attention or actually fall asleep while driving.

To avoid drowsy driving:

▸ Get plenty of quality sleep before a trip.

▸ Avoid alcoholic beverages and heavy foods.

▸ Beware of medications that can impair your driving ability.

▸ Limit long distance driving. Stop at least every two hours for rest.

▸ Stop at a safe place and take a nap. As little as 10 to 20 minutes of sleep can make a big difference.

▸ If possible, drive with a companion and switch drivers when necessary. Always let a well-rested person drive.

▸ Avoid driving from 10 p.m. to 6 a.m.

Rolling down a window, chewing gum, turning up the radio, or consuming caffeine, energy drinks or other stimulants do not prevent drowsy driving and are not reliable methods for staying awake. Drowsy driving is a type of impaired driving and puts the driver and everyone else on the roadway at risk for harm. If you observe a drowsy driver, find a safe place to stop or ask a passenger to call law enforcement. Be able to describe the location, vehicle and actions you observed.

Drinking and Driving

Legally, drivers age 21 or older are considered to be driving under the influence (DUI) if your blood alcohol content (BAC) is .08 percent or higher. If your driving is impaired, you can be convicted of driving under the influence with a BAC lower than .08 percent. If under age 21, you can be convicted of illegal consumption of alcohol if your BAC is at least .02 but less than .08. If your BAC is .08 or higher you could be convicted of a DUI. If your driving is impaired because you are under the influence of any drug, you may face the same penalties as driving under the influence of alcohol.

Researchers estimate that between the hours of 10 PM and 2 AM three out of every ten drivers are drunk. More than

21

one-third of these drivers have been drinking at someone else's home. Nearly 50 percent of the drivers arrested for DUI are social to moderate drinkers. Don't think that it won't happen to you. In your lifetime, there's a 50-50 chance that you'll be involved in an alcohol-related crash.

Just one alcoholic drink can affect your driving ability because even a small amount of alcohol affects the brain's functions – particularly vision, judgment, and coordination.

Because alcohol affects your judgment and driving ability, your chances of being in a crash are seven times greater if you drive after drinking than if you drive sober.

Twelve ounces of beer is the same as a shot of liquor or a five-ounce glass of wine.

Only time can decrease intoxication. Coffee, cold showers or exercise will not sober you up.

Alcohol-related crashes are not accidents. They can be prevented! The only way to avoid the risks of drinking and driving is to decide before you start drinking that you are not going to drive. Remember, alcohol affects judgment. Making the decision not to drive is a lot more difficult after one or two drinks.

Drive to social events in groups of two or more and have the driver agree not to drink.

Combining alcohol with other drugs usually multiplies the effects of both and can have a disastrous effect on your ability to drive. One drink taken when you are on another drug – even an aspirin, or allergy or cold medicine – could have the same effect on your driving ability as drinking several alcoholic beverages.

Almost any drug can reduce your ability to drive safely. It's not just illegal drugs that cause problems. Many over-the-counter medications and prescription drugs for headaches, hay fever, colds, allergies or nervous conditions can cause drowsiness and dizziness. This includes syrups, drops, sprays, pills and tablets. They often affect driver alertness and slow reaction time.

Read the label before taking any drug or medicine. Look for warnings about side effects. If you're uncertain about the effects of a drug, ask your pharmacist or doctor for advice. Remember that, while the effects may vary among users, no drug is harmless.

Traffic Crashes

If you are involved in a traffic crash, you must:

▶ **stop** at the scene of the crash or as close to the scene as possible without blocking traffic. Drivers must move vehicles from the road immediately if the vehicles are

able to be moved, no one is injured and the driver is capable of safely doing so.

▶ **be careful** when exiting your vehicle. Keep your vehicle between you and moving traffic if possible.

▶ **give any help** you can if someone is injured. Do not attempt to move an injured person from a wrecked vehicle unless you have the necessary medical training or there is an immediate danger such as fire.

▶ **report the crash** to the police as quickly as possible. Motor vehicle crashes involving property damage, personal injury or death must be reported to the police.

▶ **exchange information** with other people involved in the crash as soon as possible. Be sure to get the following information:

  ▶ name, address and driver's license number of other drivers

  ▶ license plate numbers of other vehicles

  ▶ name and address of anyone who was injured

  ▶ name and address of each witness

  ▶ name, address and insurance policy number of other vehicle owners

▶ **notify** your insurance company immediately.

Law enforcement officers are required to forward a written crash report to DMV when a traffic crash results in injury or the death of any person or total property damage is in excess of $1,500. All crash information will be recorded on the DMV records of each driver involved in the crash.

You must make a reasonable effort to find the owner of an unattended vehicle or other property damaged in a crash. If you cannot locate anyone, leave a note that can be found easily at the scene of the crash. Include your name, telephone number, the date and time of the crash, and a description of the damage. You must also report the crash to the police within 24 hours.

Deer Hazards

Thousands of deer-vehicle crashes take place in Virginia each year, resulting in fatalities, injuries and costly vehicle damage. To avoid hitting a deer:

▶ Be alert at dusk and dawn especially in the fall.

▶ Slow down if you see a deer near or crossing the road. Deer frequently travel in groups; there are likely more deer nearby.

▶ Use the horn to scare deer away.

▶ If a collision with a deer or other animal is unavoidable, do not swerve. Brake firmly, stay in your lane, and come to a controlled stop.

If you hit a deer, report it to law enforcement.

Traffic Stops

If you are stopped by a police officer:

► Remain calm.
► Pull your vehicle to the side of the road in a safe location and park.
► Turn on your flashers.
► If you are pulled over at night, turn on your vehicle's interior lights.
► Turn off your engine, radio, and any other device that could block communication with the officer.
► Roll down your window so that you can communicate with the officer. An officer may approach your vehicle on the driver or passenger side for safety reasons.
► Keep your safety belt fastened and ask your passengers to keep their belts fastened.
► Stay in your vehicle. Do not get out unless the officer asks you to.
► Keep your hands in plain view, preferably on the steering wheel. Ask your passengers to keep their hands in plain view also.
► Do not make any movement that will make the officer think you are hiding or reaching for something.
► Carry proper identification: a valid driver's license, proof of vehicle registration and proof of insurance. If the officer asks for these documents, tell him where they are and reach for them slowly, keeping one hand on the steering wheel.
► If the officer is driving an unmarked car or is not in uniform, you may ask to see his or her identification.
► Answer the officer's questions fully and clearly. If you disagree with the officer, do not discuss your point of view at that time. You will have your chance to make your case in court.
► You will be asked to sign the citation. Sign the citation; this is not an admission of guilt. Refusal to sign the citation may result in your arrest. Or, you may be required to go to the police station.

Section 4:
Seat Belts, Air Bags and Child Safety Seats

In this section you'll learn about:
► Seat belts
► Air bags
► Child safety seats

Wearing seat belts, also called safety belts, can double your chances of surviving a crash and more than double your chances of avoiding serious injury.

Seat Belts

Under Virginia law, the driver and all front seat passengers must wear safety belts. A driver transporting anyone younger than age 18 must ensure that the passenger is properly secured in a safety belt, booster seat or child safety seat no matter where the child is seated in the vehicle.

Remember to wear your lap belt low on your lap and against your thighs. Wear your shoulder belt over your shoulder and across your chest. Never wear your shoulder belt behind your back or under your arm. Your shoulder and lap belts should be snug. Pregnant women are much safer if buckled up by wearing the belt as low on the pelvis as possible.

Exception: A waiver of the seat belt requirement may be granted by a licensed physician if the use of a safety belt is not reasonable due to the driver's or passenger's physical or medical condition. The person granted the waiver must carry the physician's signed written statement identifying the person with the waiver and the reason for the waiver.

23

Air Bags

Air bags, when used properly with safety belts, cushion drivers and passengers as they move forward in a front-end crash. By providing a cushion, the air bag keeps the head, neck and chest from hitting the steering column or dashboard, and reduces the force of impact.

If your vehicle is equipped with air bags:

▸ Always buckle up and have all passengers in the vehicle buckle up.

▸ Move your seat back so that you are at least ten inches from the steering wheel.

▸ If your steering wheel is adjustable, tilt it downward. This points the air bag toward your chest instead of your head and neck.

▸ Children ages 12 and under are safer buckled up in the back seat.

For more information about air bags, including applying for an on/off switch, contact the National Highway Traffic Safety Administration (NHTSA) at www.nhtsa.dot.gov or toll-free hotline at 1-800-424-9393.

Child Safety Seats

Securing a child in a correctly installed child safety seat can significantly reduce the possibility of death or injury.

All children under age 8 must be properly secured in a child safety seat or booster seat when riding in vehicles manufactured after January 1, 1968. Children should ride rear facing from birth to 2 years, or as long as the safety seat manufacturer allows. If the vehicle does not have a back seat, a rear facing child seat may be placed in the front passenger seat if the vehicle is not equipped with a passenger side air bag or if the passenger air bag is turned off. Children should ride facing forward in a child safety seat or booster seat until at least age 8, or until they can attain a proper seat belt fit.

Criteria for sitting without a booster seat:

▸ Lap belt lies snugly across the upper thighs

▸ Shoulder belt lies snugly across the shoulder and chest

▸ Tall enough to sit without slouching

▸ Able to keep knees naturally bent over the edge of the vehicle seat

▸ Able to sit all the way back against the vehicle seat back

▸ Able to keep feet flat on the floor

▸ Able to sit this way for entire trip

A waiver of the child restraint law may be granted by a licensed physician if using a child restraint would be unreasonable due to the child's weight, physical fitness or other medical reasons. The person responsible for transporting this child must carry the signed written statement by the physician identifying the child and stating the grounds for the waiver.

The driver is responsible for making sure that children are properly secured. If you are convicted of violating the child restraint law, you will be fined $50. A second or subsequent offense could mean a $500 penalty.

When traveling with children:

▸ The safest place to install a child safety seat is in the center of the back seat.

▸ Numerous child safety seat checks are held in localities across Virginia. Attend one of these checks to make sure that your child's safety seat is installed correctly. Visit www.vdh.virginia.gov for more information.

▸ Never hold a child in your lap. In a crash, the child may be crushed between your body and the dashboard or the back of the seat.

▸ Make sure that all car doors are securely closed and locked before driving. If your car is equipped with a child safety lock, turn it on. Don't allow children to play with door handles or locks. If you must open a door, pull the vehicle off the road and come to a complete stop.

▸ Never allow children to ride in the luggage area of hatchbacks, station wagons or vans.

▸ Never leave a hatchback open when a child is riding in the back seat.

▸ It is illegal to transport children under age 16 in the bed of a pickup truck, even if equipped with a camper shell.

Section 5:
Penalties

In this section you'll learn about:

▸ License suspension

▸ License revocation

▸ Conviction-related suspensions and revocations

▸ Other DMV requirements, suspensions and revocations

   ▸ Driver Improvement Program

   ▸ Medical review program

   ▸ Insurance monitoring program

   ▸ Suspension for failing to satisfy child support-related requirements

▸ Alcohol and the law

   ▸ Administrative License Suspension

   ▸ Open alcohol containers in vehicles

   ▸ Transporting children while under the influence of alcohol/drugs

   ▸ Vehicle impoundment

   ▸ Restitution

   ▸ Alcohol related violations and penalties involving persons under age 21

If you break certain laws or

repeatedly violate the laws of Virginia, your driving privilege may be suspended or revoked by the court and/or DMV.

If your license is **suspended**, your privilege to drive has been withdrawn temporarily. You may pay the required fees and reinstate your license at the end of the suspension period. Also, you will be required to show proof of legal presence, which means you are either a U.S. citizen or legally authorized by the federal government to be in the U.S. During the suspension period, if your license has been expired for one year or more, you must show proof of legal presence and pass the two-part knowledge, road skills and vision exams to have your driving privilege reinstated.

Revocation means that your privilege to drive has been terminated. Your driving privilege may be restored if you re-apply for a driver's license and show proof of legal presence after the revocation period has passed. You must successfully complete the vision screening, two-part knowledge exam and road skills tests and pay the required fees when you re-apply.

Conviction-Related Suspensions and Revocations

The court or DMV will suspend or revoke your privilege to drive if you are convicted of any of the following offenses:

▸ operating a motor vehicle while under the influence of alcohol or drugs (DUI)

▸ injuring another person as a result of operating a motor vehicle while under the influence of alcohol or drugs

▸ operating a motor vehicle while suspended or revoked for a DUI

▸ operating a motor vehicle that is not equipped with the ignition interlock device when it is required by the court or DMV

▸ making a false statement to DMV

▸ failing to stop and identify yourself at the scene of a crash if someone has been injured or killed

▸ voluntary or involuntary manslaughter resulting from driving a motor vehicle

▸ involuntary manslaughter resulting from operating a motor vehicle while under the influence of alcohol

▸ committing a motor vehicle-related drug offense

▸ committing a felony involving the use of a motor vehicle

▸ taking a driver's license exam for another person, or appearing for another person to renew a license

▸ eluding police

The court may suspend or revoke your driving privilege if you are convicted of the following offenses:

▶ reckless or aggressive driving

▶ operating a motor vehicle without a valid driver's license

▶ driving while your license is revoked or suspended for a non-DUI related conviction

▶ refusing to take a blood/breath test when charged with driving while under the influence of alcohol/drugs

Refer to the DMV website under Reinstating Driving Privileges and Restricted Driving Privileges for information on other reasons for suspensions/revocations, requirements to reinstate your driving privilege, and eligibility for restricted driving privileges.

Other DMV Requirements, Suspensions and Revocations

Driver Improvement Program

If you are a Virginia resident, DMV is responsible for maintaining a driving record of all convictions received from the court. When convictions are added to your record, DMV assigns demerit points to traffic offenses and moving violations. DMV also monitors your driving record to see how many demerit points you receive within a 12-month and 24-month period. Convictions may be assigned three, four or six demerit points. For more information, refer to the Moving Violations and Points Assessment (DMV 115) publication available at www.dmvNOW.com or DMV customer service centers.

Under Age 18: If you are convicted of a demerit point traffic violation (or safety belt/child restraint violation) committed when you were under age 18, DMV will require that you complete a driver improvement clinic. If you do not complete the clinic within 90 days, DMV will suspend your driving privilege until you complete the clinic and pay a reinstatement fee.

After your second conviction for a demerit point traffic violation (or safety belt/child restraint violation) committed when you were under age 18, DMV will suspend your driving privilege for 90 days. Your third conviction will result in a revocation of your driving privilege for one year or until you reach age 18, whichever is longer.

Age 18 or 19: DMV will require you to complete a driver improvement clinic if you are convicted of a demerit point or safety belt/child restraint violation committed while you were age 18 or 19.

Age 18 or Older: DMV will require you to complete a driver improvement clinic if you accumulate 12 demerit points within 12 months or 18 points within 24 months. If you do not complete the clinic within 90 days, DMV will suspend your driving privilege.

If you receive 18 demerit points within 12 months or 24 points within 24 months, DMV will suspend your driving privilege for 90 days and require that you complete a driver improvement clinic.

For more detailed information on the Driver Improvement Program for juveniles and adults and the actions taken by DMV, refer to www.dmvNOW.com or A Different Kind of Crash Course (DMV 114) brochure.

Medical Review Program

DMV is responsible for making sure that drivers are able to safely operate motor vehicles. When DMV receives a report that a driver may have a physical or mental condition that affects his ability to drive safely, a medical review of the driver may be conducted. DMV is concerned about any condition that impairs the driver's:

▶ level of consciousness

▶ perception (vision)

▶ judgment

▶ motor skills

Depending upon the situation, DMV may require you to submit a medical or vision report completed by your physician and/or to pass the two-part knowledge exam and/or road skills test.

Once the medical review is completed, DMV will decide whether to:

▶ suspend your driving privilege

▶ restrict your driving privilege

▶ require you to submit periodic medical and/or vision reports, or

▶ end the medical review with no other requirements

If DMV suspends your driving privilege as a result of medical review action, you will not be required to present legal presence proof documents to reinstate your driving privilege unless required to do so for another suspension/revocation or your license expires.

Refer to the DMV publication, Medical Fitness for Safe Driving (MED 80), for more detailed information on the Medical Review Program.

Insurance Monitoring Program

DMV is responsible for making sure that all owners of vehicles with a valid registration comply with the Virginia laws on insurance requirements. When registering a motor vehicle, you must sign a statement on the registration application that you have liability insurance coverage for your motor vehicle, or pay the $500 uninsured motor vehicle fee. DMV will suspend your driving privilege if:

▸ you do not submit the requested insurance policy information to verify that you have liability insurance coverage

▸ there is a break in your insurance policy coverage and you do not return your license plates to DMV

Refer to www.dmvNOW.com for more detailed information on Insurance Monitoring activities by DMV.

Suspensions for Failing to Satisfy Child Support-Related Requirements

The Division of Child Support Enforcement will direct DMV to suspend your driving privilege if you:

▸ are late making child support payments by 90 days or $5,000, or

▸ fail to appear in court or comply with a subpoena, summons or warrant related to paternity or child support hearings

Refer to the DMV website under Reinstatement for information on eligibility for restricted driving privileges and requirements to reinstate your driving privilege.

Alcohol and the Law

If you are arrested for drinking and driving, the penalties are severe. If the police have probable cause to stop you and suspect that you have been drinking or using drugs, they will ask you to take a breath or blood test. Under implied consent laws, if you operate a motor vehicle on Virginia's public roads, you agree to take a breath test upon request. If you are involved in a motor vehicle crash and a law enforcement officer has probable cause, you can be arrested for DUI within three hours of the crash without a warrant and at any location.

Administrative License Suspension

If you refuse a breath test or your BAC is .08 percent or higher while you are driving and law enforcement charges you with driving while under the influence of alcohol/drugs, your driving privilege will be automatically suspended:

▸ for seven days, for a first offense

▸ for 60 days or until you go to trial, whichever comes first, for a second offense

▸ until the trial, for a third DUI offense

If you are convicted of DUI, the court and DMV will impose a suspension/revocation and other penalties in addition to the administrative license suspension. If you receive multiple DUI convictions, the suspension/revocation periods will run consecutively.

Open Alcohol Containers in Vehicles

You may be charged with drinking while operating a motor vehicle if you:

▸ are stopped by law enforcement and you have an open container of alcohol in the passenger area and the contents have been partially removed, and

▸ show signs that you have been drinking

The passenger area means the area that seats the driver and passengers and any area within the driver's reach, including an unlocked glove compartment.

Transporting Children While Under the Influence of Alcohol/Drugs

Conviction of any DUI offense involving a juvenile passenger (age 17 or younger) in the vehicle at the time of the offense carries an additional mandatory five-day jail term plus all other fines and jail sentences. You may also be charged an additional fine of at least $500 and up to $1,000. A second DUI offense with a juvenile in the vehicle carries an additional 80-hour community service requirement plus all other fines and jail sentences.

Vehicle Impoundment

Your vehicle will be impounded immediately for 30 days if you are caught driving after your license has been suspended for an alcohol-related offense. The court can impound the vehicle for an additional 90 days if you are convicted.

Also, your vehicle will be impounded by law enforcement if you operate a motor vehicle without a license after you have previously been convicted of driving without a license. The vehicle will remain impounded until you obtain a license or for three days, whichever is less.

Restitution

Depending on the laws of the city or county in which you are driving, you may be responsible for paying the cost (up to $1,000) for law enforcement, emergency medical services, fire fighters and rescue personnel who respond to a crash or incident resulting from your DUI violation.

Alcohol Related Violations and Penalties Involving Persons Under Age 21

Purchasing/Consuming Alcohol: If you are under age 21, you cannot purchase, possess or consume alcohol. If you are convicted of driving after illegally consuming alcohol, and your BAC was at least .02 percent and less than .08 percent, the court penalty will include:

▸ a suspension of your driving privilege for one year from the date of conviction, and

▸ a minimum mandatory fine of $500, or

▸ the requirement that you complete at least 50 hours of community service.

If you are convicted of driving after illegally consuming alcohol and your BAC was .08 percent or higher, you may face the same penalties as an adult.

Providing Alcoholic Beverages: If you provide or sell alcoholic beverages to a person under age 21 or someone who is intoxicated or ordered by a court to refrain from drinking alcohol, you are subject to a fine up to $2,500, mandatory suspension of your driver's license for up to one year, and 12 months in jail.

Misrepresentation of Age: If you are under age 21 and you use or attempt to use a fake ID to establish a false age in an attempt to drink or purchase alcohol, you will:

▸ be fined at least $500

▸ be required to perform at least 50 hours of community service

▸ face up to 12 months in jail, and

▸ face mandatory suspension of your driver's license for at least six months but not more than one year

Section 6:
License Types

In this section you'll learn about:

▸ Learner's Permit

▸ Driver's License

▸ Commercial Driver's License

▸ School Bus Driver's License

▸ Motorcycle Learner's Permit

▸ Motorcycle Driver's License

▸ International Driver's License

Whenever you drive, you must carry a valid driver's license or learner's permit with you. Any misuse of your driver's license or learner's permit is illegal. You could be fined, sentenced to jail, or your license may be suspended.

Learner's Permit

A learner's permit allows you to operate a motor vehicle when a licensed driver at least 21 years of age is seated in the front passenger seat. The driver with you must hold a valid driver's license, be alert and able to assist you while you are driving. The licensed driver with you may be age 18, 19, or 20 if he or she is your legal guardian, brother, sister, half-brother, half-sister, step brother or stepsister. If you are age 19 or older, you must hold a learner's permit for 60 days, or present a driver's education certificate of completion to apply for a driver's license. For more information about obtaining a learner's permit, refer to the Parents in the Driver's Seat (DMV 16) publication available at www.dmvNOW.com and DMV customer service centers.

Driver's License

A driver's license allows you to operate any vehicle or small truck less than 26,001 pounds that is exempt from commercial driver's license (CDL) requirements. Virginians have the option to obtain a REAL ID compliant driver's license. October 1, 2021, the federal government will require a REAL ID compliant credential (or another form of approved identification) to board a domestic flight or to access secure federal facilities. REAL ID compliant credentials display a small star in the upper right corner to indicate they meet federal requirements. For more information about obtaining a driver's license, refer to the publication Obtaining a Virginia Driver's License or Identification Card (DMV 141) available at www.dmvNOW.com or DMV customer service centers.

Commercial Driver's License

A commercial driver's license (CDL) allows you to operate tractor-trailers, passenger buses, tank vehicles, school buses for 16 or more occupants (including the driver), or vehicles carrying hazardous materials. For more information about CDL, refer to the Commercial Driver License Manual (DMV 60V and DMV 60A) available at www.dmvNOW.com under forms or any DMV customer service center.

School Bus Driver's License

If you wish to operate a school bus designed to carry 15 occupants (including the driver), you do not need to obtain a commercial driver's license. However, you will need to take the commercial driver and school bus tests to obtain the school bus endorsement on your driver's license. You will be restricted to driving a bus designed to carry 15 occupants (including the driver). This restriction will be printed on your license. For more information about licensing requirements to operate larger school buses, refer to Commercial Driver License Manual (DMV 60V and DMV 60A) available at www.dmvNOW.com under forms or any DMV customer service center.

Motorcycle Learner's Permit

A motorcycle learner's permit allows you to operate a motorcycle after 4 AM and before midnight. You may operate the motorcycle only when supervised by a person who is at least 21 years of age, licensed to operate a motorcycle, and able to assist you while they are supervising from another motorcycle or other vehicle riding along with you. No one, other than the operator, can be on the motorcycle. You must always wear an approved helmet while operating a motorcycle in Virginia. For more information, refer to the Virginia Motorcycle Operator Manual (DMV 2), available at www.dmvNOW.com or DMV customer service centers.

Motorcycle Driver's License

If you operate a motorcycle in Virginia, you must hold a valid motorcycle classification designation on your driver's license, or have a driver's license restricted to the operation of a motorcycle. When applying for a new motorcycle classification, riders will be asked to indicate the type of motorcycle they wish to operate, two-wheeled or three-wheeled. The appropriate classification, M2 for two-wheeled or M3 for three-wheeled, will be marked on the license once DMV staff determines the applicant has passed the road test on the type of motorcycle he/she has indicated or has completed an acceptable motorcycle rider training course. Riders who test on both two-wheeled and three-wheeled motorcycles or complete training courses for both types of vehicles will receive an M classification. An M classification signifies that the license holder is permitted to operate two-wheeled and three-wheeled motorcycles. For more information, refer to the Virginia Motorcycle Operator Manual (DMV 2)

International Driver's License

An international driver's license is not a valid driver's license and does not allow you to drive. It is only a foreign translation of your existing valid driver's license to be used when you are traveling outside of the U.S. These permits are issued by your local AAA, except to persons whose driving privilege is suspended or revoked.

If you are visiting the U.S. from a foreign country, you may drive using your driver's license issued by your home country. Your home country driver's license should be accompanied by a translation of the license.

International driver's licenses marketed by private sector businesses are not valid and do not allow you to legally operate a motor vehicle. Sale of any document claiming to be a driver's license is a Class 1 misdemeanor.

Section 7: Other Important Information

In this section you'll learn about:

▸ Receiving your license by mail

▸ Address changes

▸ New to Virginia

▸ Titles, registrations, license plates, decals

▸ Safety inspections

▸ Insurance requirements

▸ Applying to register to vote

▸ Organ, eye and tissue donation

Whether you are learning to drive for the first time, new to Virginia or brushing up on your safe driving knowledge, there are additional requirements that all Virginia drivers should know.

Receiving License by Mail

You will receive your new driver's license in the mail. For security, DMV does not issue licenses in customer service centers.

Address Changes

If you move, you are required to notify DMV **within 30 days**. The postal service will not forward your license to another address. If DMV does not have your correct address, the postal service will return the license to DMV.

New to Virginia

If you are a new Virginia resident and drive, you must obtain a Virginia driver's license **within 60 days** of moving here.

Titles, Registrations, License Plates, Decals

Title and register your vehicle and obtain Virginia license plates within 30 days of moving to Virginia. License plates must be displayed on the front and rear of the vehicle. Decals indicating the month and year that the registration expires must be placed in the designated areas on the plates (except for vehicles displaying permanent plates).

You must have the vehicle registration card with you when operating the vehicle. You must also register your vehicle in your locality, if required. Check with your city or county government.

Safety Inspections

Your vehicle must pass an annual vehicle safety inspection and display a valid safety inspection sticker. In certain localities, your vehicle also must pass an emissions inspection. For more information about Virginia safety inspections, visit the Virginia State Police website at www.vsp.virginia.gov.

Tire Safety Inspection

Once every month, or before a long road trip, check your tires for wear and damage problems by using the penny test.

1. Take a penny and hold Abraham Lincoln's body between your thumb and forefinger.

2. Select a point on your tire where the tread appears to be lowest and place Lincoln's head into one of the grooves.

3. If any part of Lincoln's head is covered by the tread, you're driving with the safe amount of tread. If your tread gets below that, your car's ability to grip the road in adverse conditions is greatly reduced.

Prior to entering the vehicle, check tire pressure using a tire pressure gauge. The recommended PSI (pounds per square inch) is located in the vehicle owner's manual or the driver's side door jamb of the vehicle.

Insurance Requirements

To register a vehicle and obtain license plates, you must have liability insurance or pay the $500 uninsured motor vehicle fee. Insure your vehicle with a company authorized to do business in Virginia. At a minimum, your insurance policy must provide the following liability insurance coverage:

Liability Insurance Coverage Requirements			
	Injury or death of one person	Injury or death of two or more people	Property damage
Policies effective before Jan. 1, 2022	$25,000	$50,000	$20,000
Policies effective on or after Jan. 1, 2022	$30,000	$60,000	$20,000

Insurance companies may factor in their policy premium the driving records of any individual of driving age that resides within an insured's household. If you have any questions regarding the potential impact a newly licensed driver may have on your policy, you may wish to contact your insurance agent.

In some cases, liability insurance requirements may be higher. Refer to www.dmvNOW.com for more information about DMV's Insurance Verification Program and Financial Responsibility Certifications.

Paying the uninsured motor vehicle fee does not provide insurance coverage, but it allows you to register and operate the vehicle in Virginia for a one-year period.

Insure your Virginia-registered vehicle during the entire registration period even if it is not driven or is inoperable. Before you cancel your insurance, return the license plates to DMV and cancel the registration.

If you are caught driving without insurance and you did not pay the uninsured motor vehicle fee, DMV will suspend your driving privilege until you:

▶ pay a $600 noncompliance fee or apply and be approved for a payment plan, and

▶ have your insurance company file a certificate that you have a policy with the required coverage limits. You will have to file this certificate of insurance for three years from the date you regain your driving privileges.

Applying to Register to Vote

You may apply to register to vote or to change your voter registration mailing address at any DMV office. Indicate your intentions on the voter registration section of the driver's license application. To apply to register to vote in Virginia, you must be a U.S. citizen, a resident of Virginia, and be at least 18 years old by the next general election. You must have had your voting rights restored by a circuit court if you have been convicted of a felony or if you have been declared mentally incompetent.

To check your voter registration status, contact your local registrar or the Department of Elections at 1-800-552-9745 or TTY 711.

Organ, Eye and Tissue Donation

To sign up to be a donor and save lives, check yes on your driver's license, learners permit, or ID card application. For more information about organ, eye, and tissue donation or to sign up online, visit www.donatelifevirginia.org.

If you are age 18 or older, your registered decision to be a donor will be honored. If you are under age 18, you can indicate your wishes to donate by checking yes; by law, your parents and guardians must make the final decision. It is important for all ages to share your decision to be a donor with your friends and family.

Section 8:
Sample Knowledge Exam

5. This road sign means:
   a. You may turn during the red light.
   b. Pass only in the right lane.
   c. One way street.
   d. Do not turn during the red light.

6. If you drive after drinking, be aware that alcohol affects:
   a. Your coordination.
   b. Your vision.
   c. Your judgment.
   d. All of these.

7. If you are driving on an icy or slippery road and have to stop:
   a. Apply brakes gently.
   b. Apply brakes in a normal manner.
   c. Keep foot off brake and let compression stop you.
   d. Press brakes firmly.

1. This road sign means:
   a. Warning of a hazard.
   b. Yield right-of-way.
   c. Railroad crossing.
   d. Speed limit.

8. The correct hand signal for stopping is:
   a. Right hand and arm pointing downward.
   b. Left hand and arm pointing straight out.
   c. Left hand and arm pointing downward.
   d. Left hand and arm pointing upward.

2. This road sign means:
   a. No U-turn.
   b. Curve.
   c. Turn right or left.
   d. Traffic flows only in the direction of the arrow.

9. When a school bus stops to load or unload children, vehicles traveling in the same direction as the bus must:
   a. Slow down and proceed with caution.
   b. Maintain speed.
   c. Stop, then proceed with caution.
   d. Stop until all persons are clear and the bus moves again.

3. This road sign means:
   a. Right lane ends soon, merge left.
   b. Soft shoulders.
   c. Low place in the road.
   d. Lane ends soon, merge right.

10. If you are involved in a crash, you must:
   a. Take the person to the nearest hospital.
   b. Continue home and file a crash report.
   c. Stop, help any injured, report the crash to the police, exchange information and notify your insurance company.
   d. Check your car for damages.

4. This road sign means:
   a. Church.
   b. First aid station.
   c. Intersection.
   d. Railroad crossing.

Answers on next page.

Notes:

Notes:

Notes:

Notes:

Notes:

Notes:

Notes:

Notes:

Notes:

Notes:

Notes:

_____

_____

_____

_____

_____

_____

_____

_____

_____

_____

_____

_____

_____

_____

_____

_____

_____

_____

_____

_____

Notes:

Notes:

Notes:

Notes:

Notes:

Notes:

Notes:

Notes:

Notes:

Notes:

Notes:

Notes:

Notes:

Notes:

Notes:

Notes:

Notes:

Notes:

Notes:

Notes:

Notes:

65

Notes:

Notes:

Notes:

Notes:

Notes:

Made in the USA
Las Vegas, NV
02 March 2024

86601671R00046